FLORA'S GEMS
The
Little Book of
DAFFODILS

Narcissus bulbocodium   Div (10)

To Sybil Christmas
Happy
love from
Ellen
x

KING ALFRED
TRUMPET   Div (1)

FLORA'S GEMS
The
Little Book of
DAFFODILS

by PAMELA TODD
Illustrated by IAN PENNEY

A Garden of
Poetry, History, Lore & Floriculture

A Bulfinch Press Book
LITTLE, BROWN AND COMPANY
Boston · New York · Toronto · London

First Edition

ISBN 0-8212-2100-0

Library of Congress Catalog Card Number 93-86020

A CIP catalogue record for this book is available from the British
Library

Conceived, edited and designed by David Fordham.

Published simultaneously in the United States of America by Bulfinch
Press, an imprint and trademark of Little, Brown and Company (Inc.),
in Great Britain by Little, Brown and Company (UK) Ltd, and in
Canada by Little, Brown & Company (Canada) Limited

PRINTED AND BOUND IN ITALY

ACKNOWLEDGEMENTS

Thanks are due for their permission to reproduce copyright material in this
volume: to The Society of Authors as literary representative of John Masefield
for 'The West Wind'; to the Estate of Colette for the extract from *For a Flower
Album* by Colette; to Martin Hopkinson Limited for the extract from *A Handbook
of Narcissus* by E. A. Bowles; to Curtis Brown London on behalf of the Estate of
Vita Sackville-West for the extract from *Vita Sackville-West's Garden Book*; to
Gerald Duckworth & Co Ltd for the extract from *Home Life* by Alice Thomas
Ellis.

The author wishes to thank Sally Kington (International Daffodil Registrar of
the Royal Horticultural Society) and the staff of the Royal Horticultural
Society's Lindley Library for their expert help and advice.

The author has used her best endeavours to clear all copyright material and
apologises in advance to any elusive authors.

CONTENTS

Above: DUTCH MASTER   *Div* (1)

PASSIONALE
LARGE-CUPPED   Div (2)

INTRODUCTION

When early primroses appear,
And vales are deck'd with daffodils,
I hail the new reviving year,
And soothing hope my bosom fills.

RICHARD WILLIAMS (1822-62)

THINK OF SPRING AND DAFFODILS COME IRRESIS-
tibly to mind. They are among the first and brightest
flowers to burst upon the scene with their buttery
yellow promise of warmth and sunshine after the drear-
iness of winter. Glimpsed gleaming in the dappled shade
of a wood during those first tentative spring days, rolling in
great yellow waves down the slope of a meadow, or simply
nodding gracefully in gregarious groups by the side of the
road, they are the colour of sunshine.

Daffodils come in an astonishing number of varieties,
from the tiny *Narcissus minimus* to large Trumpets with
flowers the size of side plates, and in a delicious range of
colours.

There is scarcely a poet in the English language who has
not celebrated daffodils, although it was Wordsworth who
immortalized them in his poem, 'I Wandered Lonely As a
Cloud'. Wordsworth first saw his great drift of daffodils
growing alongside the Lake at Ullswater during a walk with

RAINBOW
Div (2)

his sister Dorothy in 1802 and she described the sight in her journal dated 15 April:

When we were in the woods beyond Gowbarrow Park we saw a few daffodils close to the water-side. We fancied that the lake had floated the seeds ashore, and that the little colony had so sprung up. But as we went along there were more and yet more; and at last, under the boughs of the trees, we saw that there was a long belt of them along the shore, about the breadth of a country turnpike road. I never saw daffodils so beautiful. They grew among the mossy stones about and about them; some rested their heads upon these stones, as on a pillow, for weariness; and the rest tossed and reeled and danced, and seemed as if they verily laughed with the wind that blew upon them over the lake; they looked so gay, ever glancing, ever changing.

It took a further two years for William Wordsworth to shape that golden moment into some of the best known and best loved lines of English poetry:

I Wandered Lonely As a Cloud

I wandered lonely as a cloud
That floats on high o'er vales and hills,
When all at once I saw a crowd,
A host, of golden daffodils,
Beside the lake, beneath the trees,
Fluttering and dancing in the breeze.

Continuous as the stars that shine
And twinkle on the Milky Way,
They stretched in never-ending line
Along the margin of a bay;
Ten thousand saw I at a glance,
Tossing their heads in a spritely dance.

The waves beside them danced; but they
Out-did the sparkling waves in glee;
A poet could not but be gay
In such a jocund company;
I gazed – and gazed – but little thought
What wealth the show to me had brought:

For oft, when on my couch I lie
In vacant or in pensive mood,
They flash upon that inward eye
Which is the bliss of solitude;
And then my heart with pleasure fills,
And dances with the daffodils.

WILLIAM WORDSWORTH (1770-1850)

Daffodils are among the oldest cultivated plants, especially valued for their early flowers. The Greek writer Theophrastus listed and described many of the earliest kinds in his *Enquiry into Plants* written around 300BC, but we now have evidence to show that they began their spread from their original home in Spain and Portugal across Western Europe to the North of England in prehistoric times. A slightly less hardy group, known as the Tazettas, were carried by man as far as Kashmir, China and Japan, and spread naturally along the shores of the Mediterranean and into Israel, where they were to be found growing in gardens many hundreds of years before the coming of Christ.

He that has two cakes of bread, let him sell one of them for some flowers of the Narcissus, for bread is food for the body, but Narcissus is food of the soul.

MOHAMMED (c.570-632AD)

Al-Himyari, an eleventh-century Spanish Muslim, reveals in his book, *Novelties in Description of the Spring*, that 'Old Pheasant's Eye' narcissus was among the flowers most commonly grown in Spanish moorish gardens. It rivalled the rose in the affections of the Arabs, who also admired Trumpet daffodils and liked to plant them under fruit trees in their gardens.

John Parkinson, apothecary to King James I, describes in his *Paradisi in Sole: Paradisus Terrestris*, or 'A Garden of

SCARLETT O'HARA
LARGE-CUPPED   Div (2)

ST PATRICK'S DAY
Div (2)

Pleasant Flowers', (1629), about ninety different kinds of daffodil and relates how these new bulbs were brought by travellers and merchants from France, Holland, Spain, Italy and North Africa. Parkinson also tackles the thorny question: what is the difference between a daffodil and a narcissus? The answer is – none. Narcissus is simply the Latin word for a daffodil, as Parkinson rather testily explains: 'Many idle and ignorant Gardeners ... doe call some of these Daffodils narcisses, when, as all that know any Latine, that Narcissus is the Latine name and Daffodill the English of one and the same thing.'

Nevertheless the Trumpet and Large cupped types are still popularly distinguished by the name daffodil and narcissus is most often used to describe the smaller, flat-faced flowers, usually derived from N*arcissus poeticus.*

The Elizabethan herbalist, John Gerard, who was said by Parkinson to have found the double daffodil growing 'in a

AUDUBON
Div (3)

poore woman's garden' writes: 'Generally all the kinds are comprehended under the name Narcissus, in English, Daffodilly, Daffodowndilly and Primrose Peereless'. In his *Herball* (1597) he described twenty-four different daffodils, reporting that 'all and every one of them are in our London gardens in great aboundance', and listed their medicinal virtues in treating everything from sunburn and splinters to coughs, colic and 'the filth of ulcers'. He even includes a cure for acne that involved consuming the roots mixed with vinegar and nettle seed, which surely only the most desperate adolescent would attempt. But desperate men take desperate measures. The Arabs used the juice of the wild daffodil, N. *pseudonarcissus*, as a cure for baldness, although this remedy has apparently quite fallen into disuse.

In medieval times, high-born ladies occasionally cultivated daffodils in their gardens as they used the yellow dye the flowers yield to tint their hair and eyebrows.

TO DAFFODILS

Fair daffodils, we weep to see
   You haste away so soon:
As yet the early-rising sun
   Has not attained his noon.
     Stay, stay,
   Until the hasting day
     Has run
   But to the evensong;
And, having prayed together, we
   Will go with you along.

We have short time to stay as you;
   We have as short a spring;
As quick a growth to meet decay,
   As you or anything.
     We die,
   As your hours do, and dry
     Away
   Like to the summer's rain;
Or as the pearls of morning's dew,
   Ne'er to be found again.

ROBERT HERRICK (1591-1674)

SINOPEL

SMALL-CUPPED   Div (3)

YELLOW
CHEERFULNESS   *Div* (4)

There is apparently no record of when the first daffodil bulbs were taken into North America, although it is likely that they arrived in the luggage and domestic effects of the early settlers. In the 1730s John Bartram, who established one of the first plant collections in the six-acre garden at his home on the Schuykill River, a few miles from Philadelphia, wrote to Peter Collinson, the English horticulturalist, to say that daffodils were plentiful and that he did not want any more.

In the far West of America daffodils were among the flowers grown in a string of twenty-one Californian missions set up to guard the Spanish dominions in Mexico 'from invasion and insult' in the mid-1840s. They were also among the spring bulbs flowering in the 'roundabout' walk created by the great American statesman Thomas Jefferson in 1809 in the sumptuous gardens of Monticello, his estate in Western Virginia.

WHITE MARVEL *Div* (4)

They also started to crop up in American poetry. Ralph Waldo Emerson (1803-82) gives them pride of place and a convenient spelling in his poem 'The Humble-Bee':

> *Aught unsavory or unclean*
> *Hath my insect never seen;*
> *But violets and bilberry bells,*
> *Maple-sap and daffodels.*

Bees and daffodils also combine in the poem 'Telling the Bees' by Emerson's contemporary, John Greenleaf Whittier (1807-92):

> *There are beehives ranged in the sun;*
> > *And down by the brink*
> *Of the brook are her poor flowers, weed-o'errun,*
> > *Pansy and daffodil, rose and pink.*

TAHITI
DOUBLE   Div (4)

THE NAMING OF DAFFODILS

When daffodils begin to peer,
With heigh, the doxy over the dale,
Why then comes in the sweet o'the year,
For the red blood reigns in the winter's pale.

FROM THE WINTER'S TALE BY
WILLIAM SHAKESPEARE (1564-1616)

THE CLASSIFICATION OF DAFFODILS HAS LONG caused confusion. Early botanists from Pliny to Clusius all had different approaches. In 1629 John Parkinson was already deploring the unsystematic approach: 'There hath beene great confusion among many of our moderne Writers of plants, in not distinguishing the manifold varieties of Daffodils; for every one almost, without consideration of kinde or forme, or other speciall note, giveth names to diversify one from another . . . that very few can tell what they meane'.

Parkinson endeavours to help in the kindliest way by dividing them into Narcissus, which he called 'true Daffodils', and *Narcissus pseudonarcissus*, which he called 'bastard Daffodils', a distinction based on whether the cup was longer than the petals. He describes over one hundred varieties in his *Paradisus*, but because of his fondness for lengthy names, such as 'the great double yellow Spanish

RIP VAN WINKLE
Div (4)

bastard Daffodil', can hardly be said to have solved the problem.

It was to get worse before it got better. The Swedish botanist Carolus Linnaeus managed to confine the hundred or so forms current in 1753 to within six species in his *Species Plantarum* (1753), which in the second edition of 1762 he then spread to eleven divisions, very close to the twelve divisions we adhere to today. But at one point in the early nineteenth century the one genus Narcissus was split into sixteen separate genera, each named after mythical characters such as Ajax and Ganymede.

For gardening purposes the Royal Horticultural Society, as International Registration Authority for the genus Narcissus and publishers of the Classified List, classifies daffodils into twelve divisions.

The charming simplicity of daffodils coupled with their profusion made them the popular people's flower.

HAWERA
Div (5)

Daff-a-down-dill has now come to town
In a yellow petticoat and a green gown.
TRADITIONAL COUNTRY RHYME

Wild daffodils have been a common sight since medieval times and were given many regional names such as: Averell, Belle-blome, Bell Flower, Bell Rose, Bulrose, Butter and Eggs, Cincliffe, Chalice-flower, Churn, Daffadilly, Daffa-downdilly, Daffodilly, Daffy, Dilly, Downdilly, Easter Lily, Giggary, Glens, Gracy Day, Gregories, Hen and Chickens, Julians, Lent Cocks, Lent Lily, Lent Rose, Lentils, Lide Lily, Peerless Primrose, Queen Anne's Flowers and Yellow Crowbells. The old name Affodyl possibly originates from the Old English 'Affo dyle', meaning 'that which cometh early'. The daffodil is the traditional flower of Lent and, when mixed with the yew, which was used to symbolize the Resurrection, it became a suitable Easter decoration.

See that there be stores of Lilies,
Called by shepherds Daffodillies.

MICHAEL DRAYTON (1563-1631)

Alice Morse Earle, the turn-of-the-century American garden writer who lived in Brooklyn, New York, had a passion for 'old fashioned' flowers and described her preferences characteristically in her book *Old Time Garden* (1901):

In Daffodils I like the old fat-headed sort with nutmeg and cinnamon smell and old common English names – Butter-and-eggs, Codlins-and-Cream, Bacon and eggs.

The entry for the First Sunday in Lent, 10 March 1878, in the diary of the country clergyman, Francis Kilvert, is intensely vivid in its evocation of daffodils in Bredwardine on the Welsh border:

The morning sun was shining fair and bright as we walked up the path to the Church. There was a sweet stillness and Sunday peace about everything. Multitudes of daffodils grew about the Church, shining in the bright spring sunlight. I never saw daffodils in such numbers or so beautiful. They grew in forests, multitudes and multitudes, about the park and under the great elms, most of them in full blossom. As we went in we saw fresh groups of daffodils under the trees, golden gleam after golden gleam in the sweet sunshine. It was quite dazzling.

TRIANDUS ALBUS
TRIANDUS   Div (5)

THE TEARS OF NARCISSUS

Narcissus so himself forsook,
And died to kiss his shadow in the brook.

FROM VENUS AND ADONIS BY
WILLIAM SHAKESPEARE (1564-1616)

THE GREEK MYTH OF NARCISSUS, THE BEAUTIFUL boy who became enamoured with his own reflection and pined away from unrequited love, is well known. It comes from the third book of Ovid's *Metamorphoses* and like many of the Greek myths is a story of deep and passionate emotion, of loss, punishment, revenge and death. Narcissus was the son of Cephissus, the river-god, and Liriope, a naiad whom his father had ravished. Narcissus grew up extraordinarily beautiful but cold, completely untouched by any feelings of love, although both nymphs and boys alike fell under his spell. One who was particularly smitten was the mountain nymph Echo, who had no powers of speech except the ability to repeat the words she had last heard. Hera, Zeus's jealous consort, had punished Echo in this way for distracting her from Zeus's constant flirtation by her prattle. Luck was not on Echo's side. First she had the misfortune to cross Hera and then to fall deeply in

WINTER WALTZ   *Div* (6)

love with Narcissus, who slighted and rejected all her advances until at last she pined away to nothing more than a voice. Nemesis, the goddess of vengeance, watched this sad tale unfold and decided to punish Narcissus by making him fall in love with his image reflected in a pool of clear water. And there, transfixed by his own beauty, he too pined away leaving in his place a flower with a yellow centre, surrounded by white petals. The cup in the centre of the flower is fabled to contain the tears of Narcissus.

> *Bid amaranthus all his beauty shed,*
> *And daffadillies fill their cups with tears,*
> *To strew the laureate hearse where Lycid lies.*
>
> FROM LYCIDAS BY JOHN MILTON (1608-74)

In Greek and Roman myth the narcissus was said to be the last flower plucked by Persephone (or Proserpina) before she was carried off to the underworld by Hades (Dis):

JACK SNIPE

CYCLAMINEUS   *Div* (6)

> O Proserpina,
> For the flowers now that, frighted, thou let'st fall,
> From Dis's waggon! — daffodils,
> That come before the swallow dares, and take
> The winds of March with beauty
>
> FROM THE WINTER'S TALE BY
> WILLIAM SHAKESPEARE (1564-1616)

For the ancient Greeks the narcissus were a symbol of death, because they gave off an evil emanation, producing dullness, madness and death. In fact, the botanical name, *Narcissus*, is derived from the Greek word *narkē*, to benumb, in reference to the narcotic power of the plant. This influences the nervous system and has a soothing effect, which has been used to subdue hysteria as well as to produce sleep.

The Greeks placed narcissus bulbs for food and crowns of flowers in coffins so their dead could carry these with them when they went into the presence of the Fates and Furies – who were reputedly wreathed in narcissus – in the underworld.

> And narcissi, the fairest among them all,
> Who gaze on their eyes in the stream's recess,
> Till they die of their own dear loveliness.
>
> FROM 'THE SENSITIVE PLANT' BY
> PERCY BYSSHE SHELLEY (1792-1822)

PEEPING TOM   *Div* (6)

According to Sophocles, the goddesses wore crowns of narcissus which bloomed constantly in the moist and fragrant dew of Mount Olympus, and Homer, too, assures us that the narcissus delights heaven and earth by its fragrance and beauty.

PERSEPHONE

The Daffodils were fair to see,
They nodded lightly on the lea,
Persephone, Persephone!
Lo! one she marked of rarer growth
Than Orchis or Anemone;
For it the maiden left them both
And parted from her company.
Drawn nigh she deemed it fairer still,
And stopped to gather by the rill.
The Daffodil, the Daffodil.

BY JEAN INGELOW (1820-97)

DAFFODILS AND SUPERSTITION

When a Daffadill I see
Hanging down her head t'wards me,
Guess I may what I must be:
First, I shall decline my head;
Secondly, I shall be dead;
Last, safely buried.

ROBERT HERRICK (1591-1674)

THE DAFFODIL HAS JOINED THE LEEK AS THE national symbol of Wales and the pair are worn by loyal Welshmen on St David's Day, 1 March. According to legend, St David instructed his men to wear a leek in their hats to avoid confusion during a battle between his Welsh soldiers and the English. The battle was a glorious victory for the Welsh and so the leek was adopted as the Welsh national emblem, later joined by the daffodil when King George V wore one at his investiture as Prince of Wales in Caernarvon in 1911.

According to Welsh tradition it is lucky to find the first daffodil of the season, but unlucky to bring a single one into the house. This belief held true in Devon too where a single bloom inside the house spelled bad news for anyone who kept ducks, for there would be no ducklings that year. A single daffodil is often an odd and arresting sight, as Alice Thomas Ellis remarks:

The daffodil was out in the London garden when we left. Just the one, looking like someone who has turned up, dressed to the nines, for a glamorous party on the wrong night. You had to admire its style, for while it looked faintly foolish it also looked gallant and insouciant, prepared to stick it out in solitary splendour. I wish now that I had done the Perfect Hostess thing and bought a pot of its fellows to keep it company. I am thinking of those people who when they see a guest committing some dreadful social solecism – peas on the knife, drinking the water in the finger bowl – do likewise. Here in Wales of course there are fields of daffodils in positively Wordsworthian profusion and they look very beautiful but not nearly so touching.

FROM HOME LIFE BY ALICE THOMAS ELLIS (b.1932)

From China comes the story of a poor widow in the province of Fukien who was so touched by the hunger of a weary beggar who came to her door that she gave him her last half bowl of rice, even though she had been saving it for her idle son and had no idea where the next meal would come from. The beggar ate the rice, thanked the woman for her generosity, spat a few grains on the ground and disappeared. The next morning, much to the widow's astonishment, scores of graceful narcissus plants with delicate white petals and golden yellow centres had grown up in the spot. The sale of the flowers made the woman prosperous and the Fukien province famous. So in China the flower symbolized prosperity and benevolence.

NARCISSUS CYCLAMINEUS
CYCLAMINEUS   Div (6)

A PASSION FOR DAFFODILS

For a breeze of morning moves
*   And the planet of Love is on high*
Beginning to faint in the light that she loves
*   On a bed of daffodil sky.*
    FROM 'MAUD' BY ALFRED, LORD TENNYSON
                                                (1809-92)

THE CHERISHED PLACE DAFFODILS HAVE ALWAYS held in gardens, grand and small, was boosted in the early nineteenth century by the pioneering work of William Herbert, Dean of Manchester, an advanced thinker on natural history, he became convinced that many of the varieties of daffodils his fellow botanists were treating as species were, in fact, natural hybrids. To satisfy his curiosity, he began making crosses between flowers of the Trumpet, Incomparabilis and Poeticus divisions and published his findings in the *Botanical Register* (1843), adding:

It is desirable to call the attention of the humblest cultivator, of every labourer indeed, or operative, who has a spot of garden, or a ledge at his window, to the infinite variety of narcissi that may be thus raised, and most easily in pots at his window, if not exposed too much to sun and wind, offering him a source of harmless and interesting amusement, and perhaps a little profit and celebrity.

PIPIT   *Div* (7)

His call was answered by men like Edward Leeds of Manchester and William Backhouse of County Durham, the first a stockbroker and the second a banker, but both keen amateur botanists who experimented with hybridizing daffodils with great success. Another, John Horsefield, a handloom weaver who lived in a small cottage in Prestwich, raised the B*icolor* H*orsfieldii* from a cross between an English Lent Lily (N. *pseudonarcissus*) that he found growing on the banks of the River Irwell, and a small bicolor (of Haworth), which was growing in his garden. Early champions of the daffodil include the three Reverends, Wolley-Dod, Ellacombe and Engleheart, the last of whom created a sensation in 1898 with 'Will Scarlett' and another in 1907 with 'Horace'. Among others of note are F.W. Burbidge, author of *The Narcissus: Its History and Culture* (1875); E.H. Krelage, the Dutch grower, whose fine trumpet 'Madame de Graaff' commanded the first high price for a daffodil bulb when it

WATER PERRY
JONQUILLA   Div (7)

was sold in 1888 for five guineas a bulb; B.Y. Morrison, the principal founder (in 1924) of the American Horticultural Society and an ardent daffodil lover; and professional growers like Guy L. Wilson, Lionel Richardson, Grant Mitsch and Jan de Graaff.

Peter Barr, founder of the firm Barr & Sons in 1861, became known as 'The King of Daffodils' through his tireless promotion of the flower. It was his swift action in setting up a syndicate to buy the Leeds and Backhouse collections that undoubtedly saved them from disappearing altogether. His botanizing expeditions to Spain, Portugal, the Pyrenees and the Maritime Alps (which continued until he was well into his seventies) recovered wild daffodils, like N. *bulbocodium* (the Hoop Petticoat) and the little snowy-white Trumpet daffodil, N. *moschatus*, many had feared lost forever.

These men are directly responsible for the ever-increasing host of hybrids we have today. New registrations now average a hundred and sixty a year and come from countries as diverse as Great Britain, America, Australia, New Zealand, Canada and Holland, as well as Latvia and Hungary.

Not everyone, however, praised their diligent and patient efforts. The genial American writer, Louise Beebe Wilder, writing in 1936 in her book *Adventures with Hardy Bulbs*, acknowledged the debt to 'the great Daffodil

HIGHFIELD BEAUTY
Div (8)

growers' who, she said, 'make a chain with links of pure gold', but wondered if the experiment was not in danger of getting out of hand:

But now, regarding the Daffodil from an artistic standpoint rather than as a mathematical problem, or as an achievement, have they not gone far enough with its development? Should not there be a halt called in this race for bigger and better Daffodils? It is essentially a simple and friendly flower, gay, graceful, appealing, and when it is made bold, and huge, and brazen, it has been called out of character, degraded not improved.

The late Sir William Lawrence, after viewing the Daffodil Show (in New York) in April 1930, wrote: 'The dead perfection of the Daffodils approaches the mechanized flower; there they stood in well-drilled ranks, eyes front, not a button out of place.' They might be so many machine-made articles; they do not sound like the flowers that brought song to the throats of so many poets. Let us keep them a little faulty and wayward, wholly enchanting.

PAPER WHITE
GRANDIFLORA   *Div* (8)

Edward Augustus ('Gussie') Bowles had aired much the same concern in his book *My Garden in Spring* (1914):

I greatly dislike the huge race of trumpet Daffodils so much to the fore in some Dutch gardens. A man might almost feel nervous of looking down some of their trumpets, for fear of falling in and getting drowned in the honey, and a lifebelt or two should be hung among the beds.

Bowles went on to write A *Handbook of Narcissi* in 1934, the same year he was awarded the Peter Barr Memorial Cup, and his name, for many, has become synonymous with daffodils. His enthusiasm was first fired as a young man by the great Victorian parson-gardener Canon Ellacombe and ripened into a passion that was to prove lifelong. In 1913 he helped to start *The Daffodil Year Book*, which, despite an interruption during the First World War, has been published annually ever since. It acts as a sort of global parish magazine for daffodil enthusiasts, as well as providing a list of all the new hybrids. Reading the volume for 1939 one senses no shadow of the approaching war. The contents include reassuring articles entitled 'Reminiscences from Old Letters' by the Dutch grower E.H. Krelage, a report on 'Judging Daffodils in Tasmania' and a round-up of the national daffodil shows. Only 'Narcissus Leaf Diseases' sounds a more subdued note.

Daffodil shows were also a feature of the American gardening scene. The first was organized by the Maryland Daffodil Society in 1922 and led directly to the setting up of other societies and shows, notably the Virginia Daffodil Show, first held in 1931 in Charlottesville, and now one of the most important to be held in the United States.

A cloud, however, was looming on the horizon and threatening to dampen all this fresh enthusiasm. Richardson Wright, author of the *Practical Book of Outdoor Flowers* (1924), saw the writing on the wall:

Writing on Narcissi is like standing by the bedside of an old and trusted friend for whom there is little or no hope. Unless a miracle happens at Washington (of which there are no signs!) Narcissi will be excluded from the country in two years. It has a worm, it seems, and as only the physically perfect may land on these shores, it must be kept away. It was bad enough when innocuous drink was excluded, but a prohibition on Narcissi will be a tragedy.

MINNOW
TAZETTA   *Div* (8)

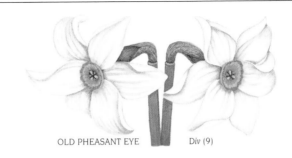

OLD PHEASANT EYE   *Div (9)*

The embargo lasted fifteen years. Instead of years of daffo-dil famine though, they marked a time of new American self-reliance. American daffodil production began in farms set up in New Jersey, the Carolinas, Florida, Michigan and California, with varying degrees of success. Those with the best natural conditions, in Long Island, Virginia, Seattle and Oregon, prospered though and, in a complete turn-about, daffodil bulbs for forcing started to be shipped to Europe.

The American passion for daffodils is still spread chiefly by the contagious enthusiasm of amateurs. In 1955 a national American Daffodil Society was formed to con-solidate the burgeoning regional societies in Indiana, Arkansas, Middle Tennessee and Southern California. It had the strong support of B.Y. Morrison, the founder of the American Horticultural Society and editor of the first five American *Daffodil Year Journals*. Morrison, who died in 1966, was an ardent daffodil lover and received numerous awards for his work, including the Gold Medal of the American Daffodil Society. Thanks to him and others there is no danger of daffodils disappearing from the American view.

> Alter? When the hills do. Surfeit? When the daffodil
> Falter? When the sun Doth of the dew:
> Question if his glory Even as herself, O friend!
> Be the perfect one. I will of you!
>
> EMILY DICKINSON (1830-86)

The English author of *Lark Rise to Candleford*, Flora Thompson, also had a passion for daffodils. In the 1920s she wrote a weekly column for the magazine *Catholic Fireside*, entitled 'The Peverel Papers':

[Daffodils] are my especial pride and delight. I watched the first green spears shoot up in February, knew when the first bud appeared, was sorry when the rain beat them down to earth, and glad when the sun coaxed them upright. Now they are out in full beauty, a long yellow pool, like sunshine spilt beneath the trees on the farther shore of the lake. I could gather whole sheaves of them if I wished without leaving the slightest gap; but I do not, for they look so perfect where they are that it seems a shame to bring them indoors to be parched by the fire and lamplight.

The memory of my discovery of these wild daffodils is amongst my earliest impressions of life upon Peverel.

ACTAEA
POETICUS   Div (9)

Daffodils in the Garden

It's a warm wind, and the west wind, full of birds' cries;
I never hear the west wind but tears are in my eyes,
For it comes from the west lands, the old brown hills,
And April's in the west wind, and daffodils.

From 'The West Wind' by John Masefield (1878-1967)

DAFFODILS ARE ONE OF THE EASIEST TO GROW and certainly the most popular of all spring-flowering bulbs. Current garden wisdom dictates that bulbs should be placed before the end of October, the earlier the better, to a depth of four to seven inches, and then left undisturbed to spread over the years, the miniature varieties in the rockery and the larger ones in grassland or garden borders. Do not remove the leaves until they are completely brown and do not tie them. Lift overcrowded or 'blind' clumps in June and July, and divide and plant the offsets.

Much has been written about naturalizing daffodils in grass and certainly anyone with space in their garden should consider the idea for daffodils are gregarious flowers and grow in large colonies in the wild. Masses of Poeticus cover hillsides in southern Europe and America where they have been successfully naturalized. The

MINIMUS   Div (10)

English Lent Lily (N. *pseudonarcissus*), if left alone, will form wide golden drifts across the grass often in the shade on the fringe of a wood or in open woodland. Properly planted they will last a lifetime.

The procedure is simple enough: choose a site where the grass may be left to grow long without creating an eyesore. Daffodils like a deep, moist, but not waterlogged loamy soil. A slope is fine as it will provide drainage. A sunny slope is even better.

Begin large-scale planting just after the first autumnal rains, when the soil is moderately soft and workable, but do not wait too long. Planting should be finished by the end of October.

Scatter the bulbs haphazardly and plant them where they fall. E.A. Bowles evolved his own idiosyncratic technique for this which he recorded in his A *Handbook of Narcissus* (1934):

I find a good way to obtain a natural effect in a drift is to choose the site for the nuclear group and lift the grass with a spade, laying it aside to be replaced and forking the ground into which the bulbs are to go. Then place some white wooden labels at the limits to which you wish that variety of Daffodil to stray.... Empty your bag or basketful of bulbs into the forked patch, all of them in a heap, stoop down (or better still, kneel if the grass is fairly dry and your knees are good but your clothes can only be said to have been so once) and start by picking up a bulb or two at a time and throwing them towards your labels. Take rather poor aim so that many may fall short of them and only a few reach the limiting target. Thus you will thin down your heap to the number you think the prepared patch should hold; plant those with a trowel and replace the turf. If you have such a tool as the thistle spud used on Sussex farms use it to lift a tuft of turf wherever a scattered bulb has fallen and push one in, stamping the turf down afterwards.

It is a sort of contrived casualness: the art is in making the drift look as natural as possible. When the bulbs are distributed use a trowel or a small spade and make the holes wide enough for the bulb to sit firmly on the soil. Plant large bulbs five inches deep and smaller ones, such as Poeticus and 'Horace', three to four inches deep. After flowering, pick off the dead heads to prevent seed pods forming and weakening the bulbs, but always leave the stalks and foliage to die back naturally. A mix of early and late varieties, starting with the early red and yellows and ending with very late flowers such as the 'Pheasant's Eye', will make the flowering season last for up to five weeks.

> *Perhaps you'd like to buy a flower?*
> *But I could never sell.*
> *If you would like to borrow*
> *Until the daffodil*
>
> *Unties her yellow bonnet*
> *Beneath the village door,*
> *Until the bees, from clover rows*
> *Their hock and sherry draw,*
>
> *Why I will lend until just then,*
> *But not an hour more!*
>
> EMILY DICKINSON (1830-86)

At the turn of the century daffodils had been press-ganged into service in the absurdly military ranks of the Victorians' formal flowerbeds. William Robinson, garden designer, influential writer and friend of Gertrude Jeykll, set out to liberate them with his revolutionary ideas on gardening. He wanted to get back to the refreshing informality of landscape gardeners like Timothy Nourse who, in his *Campania Foelix* (1700), wrote 'up and down let there be little Banks or Hillocks, planted with wild Thyme, Violets,

NARCISSUS PSEUDONARCISSUS
SPECIES (LENT LILY)   Div (10)

(i) CASSATA   Div (11)
(ii) FIRESTREAK   Div (11)

Primroses, Cowslips, Daffadille Lilies of the Valley, Blew-Bottles [*centaurea cyanus*], Daisies, with all kinds of Flowers which grow wild in the Fields and Woods . . . in a word let this be . . . a real wilderness or Thicket . . . to represent perpetual spring'. Another source of inspiration was Philip Miller, who, in his *Dictionary of Gardening* (1731), specified that flowers such as primroses, violets and daffodils and 'many other Sorts of Wood flowers' should be planted 'not in a strait line but rather to appear accidental as in a natural wood'.

This was what Robinson wanted, and to achieve it he introduced thousands of daffodil bulbs into areas of meadowland, so that they could flower in the grass which was later to be mown for hay. He planted thousands more in cattle tracks and hollows, just covering them with mud. He wanted to see an explosion of daffodils and describes the experiment in his book *The Wild Garden* (1870):

I never doubted that I should succeed with them, but I did not know I should succeed nearly so well. They have thriven admirably, bloomed well and regularly, the flowers are large and handsome and, to my surprise, have not diminished in size. In open, rich, heavy bottoms, among hedgerows, in quite open loamy fields, in every position I have tried them. They are delightful when seen near at hand and also effective in the picture. The leaves ripen, disappear before mowing time comes, and do not in any way interfere with farming. . . . A very delightful feature of the Narcissus meadow gardening is the way great groups follow each other in the fields. When the Star Narcissi begin to fade a little in their beauty the Poets follow, and as I write this paper we have the most beautiful picture I have ever seen in cultivation.

. . .

Five years ago I cleared a little valley of various fences, and so opened a pretty view. Through the meadow runs a streamlet. We grouped the Poet's narcissus near it, and through a grove of Oaks on a rising side of the field. We have had some beauty every year since; but this year, the plants having become established, or very happy for some other reason, the whole thing was a picture such as one might see in an Alpine valley! The flowers were large and beautiful when seen near at hand, and the effect in the distance delightful. This may, perhaps, serve to show that this kind of work will bring gardening into a line with art, and that the artist need not be for ever divorced from the garden, by geometrical patterns which cannot possibly interest anybody accustomed to drawing beautiful forms and scenes.

TRICOLLET
SPLIT CORONA (COLLAR)   Div (11)

Robinson had a strong supporter in Gertrude Jeykll, whose harmonious partnership with the young architect Edwin Lutyens meant that her radical ideas on colour and natural form in landscape gardening were becoming widely known. She, too, loved daffodils and describes their arrival in her own garden in spring in her book *Wood and Garden* (1899):

The early Pyrenean Daffodil is already out, gleaming through the low-toned copse like lamps of pale yellow light. Where the rough path enters the birch copse is a cheerfully twinkling throng of the Dwarf Daffodil (N. *nanus*), looking quite at its best on its carpet of moss and fine grass and dead leaves. The light wind gives it a graceful, dancing movement, with an active spring about the upper part of the stalk.

For the American garden writer, Louise Beebe Wilder, it was the earthy scent of the old double daffodil, which she grew in her New York garden, which so delighted her: 'Press its wad of crumpled green-gold petals to your nose,' she invites in her book *The Fragrant Path* (1937), 'and, wherever you may chance to be in the flesh, your spirit will be transported to moist and greening pasture lands, or to gardens where the brown mould has lately swallowed the last of the snow. It is a good smell.'

Neltje Blanchan, meanwhile, urged readers of her *American Flower Gardens* (1913) to throw caution to the wind and plant daffodils in great quantities.

KENELLIS
Div (12)

Both the yellow, long trumpeted daffodil and the fragrant white narcissus quickly colonize from comparatively small beginnings. A thousand poet's narcissus may be bought for five dollars or even less. Does the masculine amateur think it worth while to sacrifice a box of cigars for their possession, if need be, or the feminine gardener to trim over her last year's hat and spend the price of a new one on permanent joy? There are many ways of reconciling delightful extravagances to one's conscience.

At her garden at Sissinghurst, Vita Sackville-West planned a 'winter corner' around the winter aconite 'stuffed with little companions all giving their nursery party at the same time: N*arcissus minimus* and *Narcissus nanus*'. She had a special affection for what she called 'the tinies of the narcissus family', which she cultivated in pots as well as in the garden, and warmly recommends a number in her *Garden Book* (1968):

The *bulbocodium* or hoop-petticoat daffodil is an easy one, which you may have seen naturalized in grass almost by the acre at Wisley, and very pretty it is, small and tight-waisted, springing out into a crinoline. It does not like to be too dry, and the same may be said of *cyclamineus*, which lays its ears back as though frightened or in a tantrum, like the small cyclamens. N*arcissus triandrus albus*, called Angel's Tears, also lays its ears back. Ivory-white, about 6in. high, most delicately pretty, it will grow in broken shade, where it looks like a little ghost weeping.

In France, daffodils were championed by the novelist Colette, who called them *Jeannettes* and celebrated their early appearance in the south of Provence with characteristic style:

As for the *Grandee Jeannette*, this winds its hollow trumpet like an oliphant across the meadows, and so we call it the Trumpet Narcissus. Its family of stamens shelters at the base of its horn, deep as the foxglove's thimble, yellow as gold. Its sturdy corolla is nothing but a trap of blameless scent, washed clean by the rain, numbed by the cold and revived by the sun. From its neck flutters a ruffled slip of silk. Oh, this *Jeannette*, no one has ever been able to teach it to tie its cravat correctly! This does not prevent it from being the one and only bloom favoured by Parisian florists when, for the Easter festival, they make huge eggs of it and distribute them by the cartload through the streets.

From For a Flower Album (1959)

CLASSIFICATION OF *Narcissus*

DIVISION 1
Trumpet daffodils of garden origin: flowering time March to April. One flower to a stem; corona (or trumpet) as long as, or longer than, the petals. Examples are the yellow 'King Alfred' and the white 'Beersheba'.

DIVISION 2
Large-cupped daffodils of garden origin: flowering time mid-April. One flower to a stem; corona (or cup) more than one-third, but less than equal to the length of the petals. Examples are the yellow 'Carlton' and the white 'Silver Lining'.

DIVISION 3
Small-cupped daffodils of garden origin: flowering time early April. One flower to a stem; corona (or cup) not more than one-third of the length of the petals. Examples are the white 'Frigid' and the bicolor 'Mahmoud'.

DIVISION 4
Double daffodils of garden origin: flowering time mid-April. One or more flowers to a stem, with doubling of the petals, or the corona, or both. Examples are the yellow 'Golden Ducat' and white 'Snowball'.

DIVISION 5
Triandrus daffodils of garden origin: flowering time April to May. Characteristics of N. *triandrus* predominate: usually two or more drooping flowers with slightly reflexed petals to a stem. Examples are the yellow 'Liberty' and 'Dawn'.

TAFFETA

MISCELLANEOUS   Div (12)

DIVISION 6
Cyclamineus daffodils of garden origin: flowering time February. Characteristics of
N. *cyclamineus* predominate: one flower to a stem with drooping flowers with
long trumpets and strongly reflexed petals. Examples are the yellow 'Peeping Tom' and 'Tête-à-Tête'.

DIVISION 7
Jonquilla daffodils of garden origin: flowering time April to May. Characteristics of
the N. *jonquilla* group predominate: usually one to three flowers to a rounded
stem, cup shorter than the petals which are spreading not reflexed. The
flowers have a lovely fragrance and examples include the yellow 'Sweet-
ness' and deep yellow 'Golden Sceptre'.

DIVISION 8
Tazetta daffodils of garden origin: flowering time April. Characteristics of N. *tazetta*
group predominate: usually three to twenty flowers to a stout stem, cup
shorter than the petals which are often frilled; deliciously fragrant flowers.
Examples are 'Soleil d'Or' and 'Paper White'.

DIVISION 9
Poeticus daffodils of garden origin: flowering time May. Characteristics of the N.
poeticus group predominate: usually one flower per stem; pure white petals
with a disc-shaped cup with a green or yellow centre and a red rim; fragrant
flowers. Examples are the yellow and red cup 'Actaea' and the 'Old Pheasant's Eye'.

DIVISION 10
Species, wild variants and wild hybrids: flowering time March to April. Includes all
species and wild or reputedly wild variants and hybrids, including those
with double flowers.

DIVISION 11
Split-corona daffodils of garden origin: flowering time March to April. Corona split
usually for more than half its length.
a) Collar daffodils have the corona segments – usually in two whorls of three
– opposite the petals.
b) Papillon daffodils have the corona segments – usually in a single whorl of
six – alternate to the petals.

DIVISION 12
Miscellaneous daffodils
All daffodils not falling into any one of the foregoing divisions.